Yong Liu
劉墉 —— 中文・圖

Xuan Liu
劉軒

Yvonne Liu
劉倚帆 —— 英文

小沙彌
遇見
劉墉

Little Monk
Meets Yong Liu

日日是好日，時時是好時

　　佛教三藏經典，九千餘卷，浩如煙海，為了要讓大家能明白，佛陀說法度眾，也常引用譬喻輔以說明，給人接受，進而在生活裡實踐、受用。

　　回想我初到臺灣，為了把人間佛教帶到每個地方，常常借用廟口講演，只要我講到故事，群眾就會慢慢向我集中，故事講完之後敘述義理，大家又慢慢散去，一場講演大約兩個小時，群眾就像潮水一樣來來去去，都要好幾回合。

　　我從那裡學到一個經驗，人人愛聽故事，有時要「以事顯理」，有時要「以理明事」，理事要圓融，要契理契機，只有將故事與佛理結合，才是最好的弘法講演。這也是我後來一直很用心佛經裡的故事，或重視人間社會生活小故事的原因。

　　所謂「小沙彌不可輕，將來成為大法王；小兒童不可輕，將來是國家棟梁」，遠足文化出版的《小沙彌遇見劉墉》是劉墉先生結集二十篇小沙彌的故事。藉由老和尚的佛法、人生經驗，以簡短巧妙的譬喻教導小沙彌，引導閱讀者擁有正確的人生觀，在面對多變的現實生活，不致迷失方向，以智慧跳脫困境，得到解脫自在。

　　劉墉先生兼具多種身分，他是名作家，也是畫家，更是一位熱心公益的文化人，他對生命的熱愛，對生活的熱情，從《小沙彌遇見劉墉》這本書可見一斑。每篇文章搭配彩色水墨畫，柔和細膩的色調，加上活潑生動的布局，增強故事的張力，讓閱讀者多了圖像的思考空間，相信大家一定會很喜愛。我非常樂見它的出版並且向大家推薦。

　　是為序。

星雲

二〇二〇年三月　於佛光山開山寮

Every Day Is a Good Day, Every Hour Is a Good Hour

With the Tripitaka and more than 9,000 other volumes, Buddhist teachings are as vast as the sea. To help everybody understand, the Buddha lectured on doctrines to enlighten crowds, and he also utilized descriptive analogies, which people could accept and then practice and benefit from in everyday life.

Thinking back to when I first arrived in Taiwan, in order to bring Humanistic Buddhism to all places, I frequently lectured at temple gates. When I told stories, the crowds gradually gathered around me. When I finished the stories and spoke about theories, people gradually dispersed. Each lecture was approximately two hours, and the crowds came and went like tides, multiple times.

I learned from that experience that all people love to listen to stories. Sometimes, we need stories to demonstrate principles; other times, we need principles to explain stories. Principles and stories must round each other out, while being true both to teachings and to humans' hearts. Combining stories and principles is the only way to give the best kind of Buddhist lecture. This is why since then I have always been very attentive to the stories in the Buddhist scriptures and to the little stories in human societies and everyday lives.

We similarly say: "Don't underestimate the little monk, for he can later become the great master; don't underestimate the small child, for he can later be the beam holding up the country." Published by Walkers Cultural Enterprise Ltd., *Little Monk Meets Yong Liu* is Mr. Yong Liu's compilation of twenty Little Monk stories. Through the old Master's Buddhist teachings and life experience, he uses simple clever analogies to teach the Little Monk. This guides readers to have a correct outlook on life and, when facing the ever-changing realities of life, to not lose one's direction but rather use wisdom to overcome obstacles and achieve the relief of freedom.

Mr. Yong Liu has many identities. He is a famous writer, and he is also an artist. He is furthermore a public-spirited man of culture. His love of life and his enthusiasm for living can be clearly seen in this book, *Little Monk Meets Yong Liu*. Every story is paired with a watercolor and ink drawing, of delicate and exquisite colors and lively and vivid composition, which increases the story's tension and gives readers a visual space for imagination. I believe everyone will really enjoy this book. I am very happy to see it published, and I recommend it to all.

This is the foreword.

Hsing Yun

Fo Guang Shan Institute of Humanistic Buddhism, March 2020

劉爺爺說故事

　　我在臺北跟兒子住得很近，兒子和兒媳婦一有應酬，我就去監督孫子孫女吃飯。這是我很樂意做而且引以為傲的，因為在我的監督之下，兩個小鬼比他們父母在家時吃得快。我用的方法是「故事配飯」，只要我開講，兩個小鬼會瞪大眼睛聽。他們不好好吃，我就不往下講，為了繼續往下聽，十歲的孫女和八歲的孫子總會大口地把飯吃完。

　　我很愛寫故事、說故事，會為大人寫《冷眼看人生》和《我不是教你詐》，也會為青少年寫《點一盞心燈》和《捕夢網》，因為我發現說故事是最好的教育方法，它不生硬、不教條，能夠把很深的道理，用引人入勝的方式傳達。

　　這本書裡收納了我過去五十年間寫的小故事，雖然主角只有小沙彌跟老師父，但是完全沒有宗教性，我只是藉著一對師徒，說些人生的道理。因為文字淺、寓意深，七八歲的小孩能聽得懂，七八十歲的讀者也能發會心的一笑。

　　書裡的插圖都是我親自繪製的，有人笑我把「畫大畫」的時間拿來作「小孩書」，豈知「邊寫邊畫」是我人生最大的樂事。

　　英譯由倚帆和劉軒完成，其中很多故事是他們小時候聽過的，除了更能心領神會，還重溫了童年往事，希望這本書也能帶給更多人快樂的時光。

二〇二〇年三月

Storytime with Grandpa Liu

I live very close to my son in Taipei. When my son and daughter-in-law aren't home for dinner, I go over to supervise my grandson and granddaughter as they eat. This is something I am glad to do and proud to do because, under my supervision, the two little monsters eat faster than when their parents are home. My method is "stories with rice." When I tell a story, they listen with widened eyes. If they don't eat what they should, then I stop telling the story. For me to continue the story, my 10-year-old granddaughter and 8-year-old grandson always take big bites to finish their meal.

I love to write stories and tell stories. I've written *A Hard Look at Humanity* and *I'm Not Teaching You to Be Conniving* for adults, and I've written *Light the Lamp in Your Heart* and *Dreamcatcher* for young adults. I've realized that telling stories is the best way to teach. Stories are neither rigid nor dogmatic; they can communicate profound philosophy in a fascinating manner.

This book compiles short stories that I have written over the past 50 years. Although the main characters are a Little Monk and his old Master, this book is not meant to be religious. I am merely demonstrating life philosophies through the relationship of master and apprentice. The word choice is simple, while the morals of the stories are deep. Seven- or eight-year-old children can understand, and 70- or 80-year-old readers can also knowingly smile.

I personally drew all the illustrations in this book. Some people joke that I use time that could be used on great paintings to instead produce a book for little ones. What they don't know is that writing and drawing at the same time is one of the greatest joys of my life.

The English translations were done by my daughter Yvonne and my son Xuan. They had heard me tell many of these stories when they were younger, and so they very well understand the unspoken meanings behind the words. These stories refresh their childhood memories, and we hope this book brings joy to more people.

Yong Liu

March 2020

小沙彌
遇見
劉墉

Little Monk
Meets Yong Liu

放下 · 放空 · 放平 · 放心 · 放手

To Give

小沙彌對什麼都好奇。秋天，禪院裡紅葉飛舞，小沙彌跑去問師父：「紅葉這麼美，為什麼會掉呢？」

師父一笑：「因為冬天來了，樹撐不住那麼多葉子，只好捨。這不是『放棄』，是『放下』！」

Little Monk was new to the monastery and curious about everything.

In autumn, red foliage fluttered in the monastery yard. Little Monk asked Master, "These leaves are so beautiful. Why do they fall?"

Master smiled. "Winter is coming, and the tree cannot hold on to so many leaves, so it must choose. The tree is not giving up; rather, it is choosing to give away."

冬天來了，小沙彌看見師兄們把院子裡的水缸扣過來，又跑去問師父：「好好的水，為什麼要倒掉呢？」

師父笑笑：「因為冬天冷，水結凍膨脹，會把缸撐破，所以要倒乾淨。這不是『真空』，是『放空』！」

大雪紛飛，厚厚地，一層又一層，積在幾棵盆栽的龍柏上，師父要小沙彌幫忙把盆搬倒，讓樹躺下來。

Winter arrived. Curious Little Monk saw elder monks turning over the water barrels one by one. He asked Master, "There is still good water in many of the barrels. Why must we pour the water out?"

Master smiled. "When the water freezes, it will crack the barrels, so we must pour all the water out. We are not depleting the barrels; rather, we are unloading them."

A blizzard came, sweeping piles of thick snow onto the junipers. Master asked Little Monk to help him tip the potted saplings over.

小沙彌又不解了，急著問：「龍柏好好的，為什麼弄倒？」

師父臉一整：「誰說好好的？你沒見雪把柏葉都壓塌了嗎？再壓就斷了。那不是『放倒』，是『放平』，為了保護它，教它躺平休息休息，等雪霽再扶起來。」

天寒，加上全球金融危機，香油收入少多了，連小沙彌都緊張，跑去問師父怎麼辦？

Little Monk was confused. "Aren't the saplings doing fine? Why lay them down?"

Master replied sternly: "Who says they're doing fine? Don't you see how the snow is weighing them down? By laying the saplings down, we are protecting them, so that they may stand again after the snow. We are not forcing them to fall over; rather, we are teaching them to rest."

The winter was harsh and long, and with a global recession, the monastery's offering box was running empty. Even Little Monk felt nervous and asked Master what to do.

「少你吃？少你穿了嗎？」師父瞪一眼：「數數！櫃裡還掛了多少衣服？柴房裡還堆了多少柴？倉房裡還積了多少糧食？別想沒有的，想想還有的；苦日子總會過去，春天總會來到。你要放心。『放心』不是『不用心』，是把心安頓。」

"Have you been eating or wearing less?" Master replied with a glare. "Go see for yourself, how many clothes are there in the closet? How many piles of firewood are there in the shed? How many bags of rice and grain are there in the barn? Stop thinking about what we don't have, and think about what we do have. The hard times will pass, and spring will come. You need to trust. This does not mean you stop being mindful; rather, you calm your heart with trust."

春天果然跟著來了，大概因為冬天的雪水特別多，春花爛漫，更勝往年，前殿的香火也漸漸恢復往日的盛況。師父要出遠門了，小沙彌追到山門：「師父您走了，我們怎麼辦？」

師父笑著揮揮手：「你們能放下、放空、放平、放心，我還有什麼不能放手的呢？」

Spring indeed arrived, and the thawing snow made for even more blossoms than last year. Worshippers returned, and the offering box became full again. It was then that Master prepared to set off on a long journey. Little Monk ran up to him at the mountain gate. "Master! When you are gone, what are we to do?"

Master smiled and waved his hand. "You have already learned how to give away, to unload, to rest, and to trust. Is there any reason why I should not let go?"

放，不是放棄、不是放任、不是放恣、不是放縱、不是放逐。

不曾拿起，怎麼放下？
不曾擁有，怎麼放空？
不曾獨立，怎麼放平？
不曾掛念，怎麼放心？
不曾抓緊，怎麼放手？

有收才能放，有放才能收！

Letting go is not letting alone, and it is not giving up. It does not indulge with abandon, nor does it abandon through rejection.

If you do not pick up, then how can you give away?
If you do not acquire, then how can you unload?
If you do not strive, then how can you rest?
If you do not care, then how can you trust?
If you do not hold on, then how can you let go?

Just as you need to take in order to give, you must give in order to take!

天地禪院

The Temple Between Heaven and Earth

小沙彌坐在地上哭，四周都是寫了字的廢紙。

「怎麼啦？」師父問。

「寫不好。」

師父撿起幾張看：「寫得不錯嘛，為什麼扔掉？又為什麼哭？」

Little Monk sat on the floor, crying. All around were discarded papers with writing on them.

"What's the matter?" Master asked.

"I can't write well."

Master glanced at a few pages. "They are not bad! Why discard them? And why cry about it?"

「我就是覺得不好。」小沙彌繼續哭：「我喜歡完美，一點都不能錯。」

「問題是，這世界上有誰能一點都不錯呢？」師父拍拍小沙彌：「你什麼都要完美，一點不滿意，就生氣、就哭，這反而是不完美了。」

"I think they are no good." Little Monk sulked. "I need perfection. I can't tolerate a single mistake."

"Well, question is, can anyone in this world never make mistakes?" Master gently patted Little Monk. "You want everything to be perfect, and if dissatisfaction makes you angry and tearful, this alone would be an imperfection."

小沙彌把地上的字紙撿起來，先去洗了手。又照照鏡子，去洗臉；再把褲子脫下來，洗了一遍又一遍。

「你這是在幹麼啊？你洗來洗去，已經浪費半天時間了。」師父問。

「我有潔癖！」小沙彌說：「我容不得一點髒，您沒發現嗎？每個施主走後，我都把他坐過的椅子擦一遍。」

Little Monk picked up the papers, washed his hands, and looked in the mirror, washed his face, then took off his pants and washed them over and over.

"What are you doing? You're washing this and that, and wasting half of the day," Master said.

"I am obsessed with cleanliness!" Little Monk said. "I cannot tolerate any dirt. Have you noticed that after every guest leaves, I always wipe his chair clean?"

「這叫潔癖嗎？」師父笑笑：「你嫌天髒、嫌地髒、嫌人髒，外表雖然乾淨，內心反而有病，是不潔淨了。」

"Is this so-called cleanliness obsession?" Master chuckled. "If you are always complaining that everything and everyone is dirty, even when you look clean on the outside, your spirit will be sick and impure on the inside."

小沙彌要去化緣，特別挑了一件破舊的衣服穿。

「為什麼挑這件？」師父問。

「您不是說不必在乎表面嗎？」小沙彌有點不服氣：「所以我找件破舊的衣服。而且這樣施主們才會同情，才會多給錢。」

Little Monk set out to collect alms, wearing a set of particularly shabby clothes.

"Why did you choose to wear these?" Master asked him.

"Didn't you teach us to look past the surface?" Little Monk said with a hint of sarcasm. "That's why I wear shabby clothes. And this way, benefactors will take pity on me and donate more."

「你是去化緣，還是去乞討？」師父瞪了眼睛：「你是希望人們看你可憐，施捨你？還是希望人們看你有為，透過你度化更多人？」

"Are you collecting alms, or are you begging?" Master looked stern. "Do you want people to take pity on you, treat you as charity? Or do you want people to see promise in you, and aspire to higher spiritual purpose through you?"

師父圓寂了，小沙彌成為住持。

他總是穿得整整齊齊，拿著醫療箱，到最髒亂貧困的地區，為那裡的病人洗膿、換藥，然後髒兮兮地回山門。

Master passed away. Little Monk became the abbot.

It is said that he always dresses neatly, carrying a medical kit to the poorest slums, cleaning wounds and changing bandages for the sick before returning to the temple, soiled head to toe.

他也總是親自去化緣，但是左手化來的錢，右手就濟助了可憐人。他很少待在禪院，禪院也不曾擴建，但是他的信眾愈來愈多，大家跟著他上山、下海，到偏遠的山村和漁港。

He also personally makes the rounds to collect alms, but whatever he takes in immediately goes to help the needy. He is rarely at the temple, which hasn't expanded in years, but his followers are always increasing in number. They follow him from mountain to sea, into remote towns and fishing villages.

「師父在世的時候，教導我什麼叫完美，完美就是求這世界完美；師父也告訴我什麼是潔癖，潔癖就是幫助不潔的人，使他潔淨。師父還開示我，什麼是化緣，化緣是使人們能彼此幫助，讓眾生結善緣。」新的住持說：

「至於什麼是禪院，禪院不見得要在山林，而應該在人間。南北西東，皆是我弘法的所在；天地之間，就是我的禪院。」

"When my Master was alive, he taught me the meaning of perfection, which is to make this world as good as it can be. Master taught me that obsession about cleanliness should be applied to help those who are unclean become clean. Master also enlightened me on the meaning of alms, which is to enable people to help one another, and to bond through good deeds," said the abbot.

"And what is a temple? A temple shouldn't be secluded in mountain forests. It should be amongst the people. North, south, east, west - I carry forward the teaching of the truth. And anywhere between heaven and earth, you shall find my temple."

心上的落葉

Fallen Leaves of the Heart

深秋了，小沙彌每天忙著掃落葉，一邊掃一邊落，常常早晨才掃乾淨，下午又落滿了庭院，還得再掃一次。

「哪裡是落葉？根本是煩惱嘛！」小沙彌邊掃邊怨，正巧被師父聽到了。

It was late autumn, and Little Monk was busy sweeping leaves every day. While he swept, the leaves kept falling. It often took him all morning to sweep the courtyard clean, and by the afternoon, he had to do it all over again.

"You aren't just leaves; you're trouble!" Little Monk complained as he swept, and Master overheard him.

「你說落葉是煩惱？」師父笑問：「說得好！說得好！煩惱來了，掃掉！煩惱再來，再掃掉！」

「可是風大，還會把別處的落葉吹過來。」小沙彌指著禪院的圍牆說：「咱們的牆太矮，門又總是開著，外面的落葉會偷偷溜進來。」

「裡面的落葉不是也會被風吹出去嗎？掃落葉不必問它的來處，既然落在咱們院裡，就咱們管！」

"You say the leaves are trouble?" Master asked with a smile. "Well said, well said! When trouble comes, we sweep it away! When trouble comes again, we sweep it away again!"

"The wind is too strong. It keeps blowing in leaves from other places," Little Monk said and pointed at the monastery walls. "Our walls are too low, and our gates are always open. Fallen leaves find a way to sneak in."

"Well, don't some of our fallen leaves get blown out as well? There's no need to mind where the leaves come from. As long as the leaves are in our garden, we'll take care of it!"

師父拍拍小沙彌：「有新綠，就有枯葉；有得意，就有煩惱。今天落，今天掃；明天落，明天掃。不必因為掃了還會落，就不掃。我們心裡也有這樣的庭院，有花開就有花落，有葉生就有葉落。不怕落葉多，只要勤打掃，不疾不徐、一帚一帚，慢慢掃，掃也是一種修行。」

Master patted Little Monk gently. "Where leaves grow, leaves will fall. Where there is happiness, there is also sorrow. If the leaves fall today, then we sweep today; if the leaves fall tomorrow, then we sweep tomorrow. Although we know more leaves will fall later, we don't stop sweeping now. We have such a garden in our hearts too. Flowers bloom and wilt; leaves grow and are cast away. We do not see them as troubles, as long as we keep sweeping. Diligently, steadily, sweep by sweep, let the sweeping become your meditation."

從我們來到這個世界的那一刻，就有了不斷的相聚與別離，就有了不斷的得與失。有倉廩就難免鼠患，有子女就難免煩惱，有愛情就難免牽掛，有身體就難免病痛……

From the moment we arrive in this world, people come together and separate repeatedly; we gain and we lose repeatedly. If we harvest and store, then we inevitably suffer from rats. If we have sons and daughters, then we inevitably worry. If we love someone, then we inevitably care too much. If we have a body, then we inevitably fall ill.

師父的葫蘆

Master's Gourd

小沙彌去見師父：

「師父！我時時打坐，常常念經，早起早睡，心無雜念，沒有任何人能比我更用功了，為什麼我就是無法開悟？」

師父拿出一個葫蘆、一把粗鹽，交給小和尚：

「去裝滿水，再把鹽倒進去，使它溶化，你就開悟了！」

Little Monk went to see Master.

"Master! I meditate a lot. I recite my scriptures often. I keep early hours and stay mindful all the time. I'm pretty sure no one works harder than I do. Why am I still not enlightened?"

Master took out a gourd and a handful of coarse salt, and he gave these to Little Monk. "Go fill up the gourd with water and put in the salt. Make it dissolve immediately, and then you will be enlightened!"

過不多久，小沙彌跑了回來：

「葫蘆口太小，我把鹽倒進去，只溶化了一部分，多半沉在底下不溶化。伸進筷子又攪不動，我還是沒有辦法開悟。」

Little Monk came back to see Master shortly after. "The opening of the gourd is too small. I put the salt in, but only some of it dissolved, while the rest stays at the bottom. I tried to reach the remaining salt with a chopstick, but there's no room to stir. I am still not enlightened."

師父笑笑，拿起葫蘆倒掉一些水，只搖幾下，鹽就溶化了：

「一天到晚用功，不留點平常心，就如同裝滿水的葫蘆，搖不動、攪不得，怎麼化鹽？又怎麼開悟？」

Master smiled and picked up the gourd. He poured out some water and shook it a little, and the salt dissolved immediately. "When you study all the time but don't keep a sense of balance, you are just like this gourd filled with water: nothing shakes, nothing stirs. How can anything dissolve? When there is no room in your life, how is it possible for you to be enlightened?"

心弦

Heartstrings

師父的臥榻旁總擺著一塊長長的木板。

小沙彌好奇：「師父，您那塊木板是作什麼用的？」

「那是個沒有琴弦的古琴，師父的師父留下來的。」

「沒有琴弦怎麼彈？您為什麼不裝琴弦呢？」

「師父沒學過，不會彈。」

「那把它放在這兒幹什麼？」

There has always been a long wooden board next to Master's bed.

Little Monk curiously asked, "Master, what is the board for?"

"It is an ancient lute without strings. It was left by the Master before me," Master answered.

"How do you play it without strings? Why don't you restring it?"

"I never learned how to play it."

"Then why is it still here?"

「但識琴中趣，何勞弦上聲？手不會彈，心可以彈啊！師父每次看到它，就會想：我心裡的琴弦調音了嗎？那音準不準？我的心裡有旋律嗎？那旋律美不美？」

"Without making a sound, one can still feel the joy of playing, no? Even if you cannot play it with hands, you can still play it with heart! Every time I see it, I ask myself: Have I tuned the strings in my heart? Is the tone true? Can I hear the melody in my heart? Is the melody beautiful?"

師父摩挲著古琴說：「每個人的身體都是琴台，心裡都有琴弦，要常常調音，聲音才正；要常常撥動，才不致像塊死木頭。世間人的煩惱，常因為心裡的音亂了。做老師的人必須時時反省，先把自己心裡的琴弦調好，才能為學生調音啊！」

Master gently stroked the lute and said: "The body is like a lute. There are strings in everyone's heart. We need to keep it in tune, so that our tune stays true; we need to keep strumming, to keep the song alive. Our worries are often due to dissonance of the heart. Those who teach must be diligent in reflection to keep their heartstrings in tune, so that we may help to tune others!"

正字與反字

The Word
and the Backward

小沙彌滿懷疑惑地去見師父：

「師父！您說好人壞人都可以度化，問題是壞人已經失去了人的本質，怎麼算是人呢？既然不是人，就不應該度化他。」

師父沒有立刻回答，只是拿起筆在紙上寫了個「我」，但字是反寫的，如同印章上的文字，左右顛倒。

The puzzled Little Monk went to see his Master.

"Master, you said that everyone can become enlightened. But if a person is evil and has already lost his human nature, can he still be enlightened as a human being? I have my doubts!"

Master did not reply right away. Instead, he picked up the brush and wrote the character that means "self," except the word is flipped horizontally, as it would appear if carved on a chop.

「這是什麼？」師父問。

「這是個字。」小和尚說：「但是寫反了！」

「什麼字呢？」

「『我』字！」

「寫反了的『我』字算不算字？」師父追問。

「不算！」

「既然不算，你為什麼說它是個『我』字？」

"So, what is this?" Master asked.

"It is a word," Little Monk answered. "But backward!"

"What word is it?"

"Self!"

"Do you think this backward 'self' is still a word?" Master asked.

"No!"

"If you say it's not, then why do you still recognize it as 'self'?"

46

「算！」小沙彌立刻改口。

「既算是個字，你為什麼說它反了呢？」

小和尚怔住了，不知怎樣作答。

"Um...yes, it's a word then!" Little Monk corrected himself immediately.

"If it's a word, then why do you say it's backward?"

Little Monk did not know what to say.

「正字是字，反字也是字，你說它是『我』字，又認得出那是反字，主要是因為你心裡認得真正的『我』字；相反地，如果你原先不識字，就算我寫反了，你也分不出來，只怕當人告訴你那是個我字之後，遇到正寫的我字，你倒要說是寫反了！」

"A word is a word, even when backward. You recognize this 'self' as backward because you have an impression of a correct 'self' in your heart. On the other hand, if you were illiterate, it would make no difference if I wrote it one way or another. In fact, if you learned it this way, one day when you see the right word, you may very well claim that it's backward!" Master said.

師父說：「同樣的道理，好人是人，壞人也是人，最重要的是你要認得人的本性，於是當你遇到惡人的時候，仍然一眼便能見到他的『天質』，並喚出他的『本真』。本真顯現，就不難度化了！」

"This principle also applies to people. Whether good people or bad people, they are all people. The most important thing is to recognize their humanity. Therefore, when you meet sinful people, you can see through to their human character and call out to their authentic humanity. When their authenticity is made obvious, enlightenment is made possible!"

好好活著

Live Well

大熱天，禪院裡的花被曬蔫了。

「天哪，快澆點水吧！」小沙彌喊著，接著去提了桶水來。

「別急！」師父說：「現在太陽大，一冷一熱，非死不可，等晚一點再澆。」

傍晚，那盆花已經成了「梅乾菜」的樣子。

On a hot day, the flowers in the monastery were withering under the sun.

"My goodness! Let's hurry and water them!" shouted Little Monk, as he carried over a bucket of water.

"Don't rush!" said Master. "The sun is too strong now. Being cold one minute and hot one minute will make them die for sure. Wait until it's cooler outside to water them."

By that evening, the flowers already looked like dried pickled vegetables.

小沙彌咕咕噥噥地說：「一定已經死透了，怎麼澆也活不了了。」

「少囉嗦！澆！」師父罵。

水澆下去，沒多久，已經垂下去的花，居然全站了起來，而且生意盎然。

「天哪！」小沙彌喊：「它們可真厲害，憋在那兒，撐著不死。」

「胡說！」師父罵：「不是撐著不死，是好好活著。」

Little Monk muttered: "They must be completely dead now. No amount of water can save them."

"Stop muttering! Water!" Master scolded.

Soon after watering, the previously drooping flowers surprisingly all perked up and looked full of life.

"My goodness!" Little Monk shouted. "They are truly impressive. They held on and resisted death."

"Nonsense!" Master scolded. "They were not resisting death; they were living well."

「這有什麼不同呢？」小和尚低著頭。

「當然不同。」師父拍拍小和尚：「我問你，我今年八十多了，我是撐著不死，還是好好活著？」

晚課完了，師父把小和尚叫到面前問：「怎麼樣？想通了嗎？」

「沒有。」小沙彌還低著頭。

師父敲了小和尚一下：

"What is the difference?" asked Little Monk with his head down.

"Of course there is a difference." Master patted Little Monk. "Let me ask you: I am over 80 years old this year. Am I resisting death, or am I living well?"

After Night Prayer, Master called Little Monk over and asked: "How do you feel? Have you figured it out?"

"No," said Little Monk, still with his head down.

Master knocked Little Monk on the head.

「笨哪！一天到晚怕死的人，是撐著不死；每天都向前看的人，是好好活著。得一天壽命，就要好好過一天。那些活著的時候天天為了怕死而拜佛燒香，希望死後能成佛的，絕對成不了佛。」

師父說：「他今生能好好過，都沒好好過，老天何必給他死後更好的日子？」

"Silly! Someone who is afraid of death from morning to night is resisting death. Someone who looks to the future every day is living well. When you are blessed with another day of life, you should live well for another day. Some people always pray and burn incense because they are afraid of death and hope to achieve Buddhahood after death; they will certainly not achieve Buddhahood."

Master continued: "If a person who is able to live well in this life never lives well, then why would the heavens give him a better life after death?"

殺手的愛

A Killer's Love

小沙彌正在練字，突然聽見窗外傳來「啪」的一聲，抬頭看，是隻大螳螂落在紗窗上。

小沙彌興奮地走到窗前，貼近看。

突然「啪」一聲，又飛來一隻螳螂，居然以迅雷不及掩耳的速度，爬到先前螳螂的背上。

「專心寫字，不要看！」師父說：「深秋了，到牠們交配的季節了。」

Little Monk was practicing his penmanship when he heard a sudden "pa" sound from outside the window. He looked up and saw that a large praying mantis had landed on the window screen.

Little Monk excitedly walked to the window to take a closer look.

Suddenly there was another "pa"! A second praying mantis had flown over, and with lightning speed, it climbed onto the first praying mantis' back.

"Focus on your writing! Don't look!" said Master. "It's late autumn now, their mating season."

小沙彌定睛，果然兩隻螳螂屁股連在一塊兒，小沙彌有點不好意思，回到桌上寫字，但是一邊寫一邊偷偷看。

「不得了了！師父！」小沙彌突然放下筆喊：「牠們在打架，一隻咬另一隻，那隻居然不躲，頭都被咬掉了！」

「專心寫字！」師父沒抬頭：「牠願意被咬，就讓牠咬吧！」

Little Monk stared. The two praying mantises' butts were sure enough connected. Little Monk felt a bit shy. He went back to his desk, but he continued to peek at the window while writing.

"Oh no! Master!" Little Monk suddenly shouted as he put down his pen. "They're fighting! One is biting the other, and the one being bitten isn't even running away. His head is nearly bitten off!"

"Focus on your writing!" said Master without looking up. "One is willing to be bitten, so let the other one bite!"

「一隻欺侮一隻怎麼成呢？」小沙彌嘟著嘴喊：「還在咬！後來的那隻已經被吃掉一半了！牠怎麼不躲呢？牠疼不疼？」

「一個願吃，一個願捱。有牠們的道理，不用管！」

天漸黑，兩隻螳螂只剩一隻了，兇悍的那一隻因為吃了別人，肚子變得好大。

"How can one bully the other?" Little Monk shouted with a pouty face. "It's still biting! That second praying mantis only has half his body left! Why doesn't he run away? Does he feel pain?"

"One wants to eat, and the other wants to suffer. They have their reasons. Don't mind them!"

As the sky darkened, only one of the two praying mantises remained. The aggressive one's belly was big from eating the other one.

小沙彌有點傷心，對師父說：「不是不能殺生嗎？人不殺，野獸就可以吃野獸，蟲子就能吃蟲子嗎？牠們的吃，不是殺生嗎？」

「牠們的殺，是為了生。不殺就不能生。」師父也走到窗邊，看那隻大肚子的螳螂：「牠們是一公一母，被吃掉的是公的。」

Little Monk felt a bit sad. He said to Master: "Isn't it wrong to kill? Humans should not kill, but it's okay for animals to eat animals, and insects to eat insects? Isn't their eating a type of killing?"

"Their killing is for the purpose of living. If they don't kill, then they cannot live." Master also walked to the window and looked at the praying mantis with the big belly. "They were one male and one female. The one who was eaten was male."

小沙彌大吃一驚：「那牠們就是夫妻了，不是太太把丈夫吃了嗎？這真是太狠毒了！天理難容啊！」

師父笑笑：「母螳螂吃公螳螂也是天理，你以後就懂了！」

隔天清早，小沙彌急著跑到窗邊看。

「母螳螂不見了！」小沙彌喊。

Little Monk was shocked. "That means they were husband and wife! The wife ate her husband? That is truly brutal! That goes against natural principles!"

Master smiled. "Female praying mantises eating male praying mantises is an act of natural principle. You'll understand later!"

Early the next morning, Little Monk hurried to look out the window.

"The female praying mantis is gone!" Little Monk hollered.

「應該是去下蛋了！」師父說。

「下蛋？」小沙彌瞪大眼睛。

是啊！天就要冷了，螳螂受不了，在被凍死之前，牠會先下蛋，蛋不怕寒，隔年天暖就會跑出好多螳螂寶寶。

「可⋯⋯可是那太太又為什麼把丈夫吃掉呢？」

"She probably left to lay eggs!" said Master.

"To lay eggs?" Little Monk widened his eyes in disbelief.

"Yes! The days are getting colder, and the praying mantis cannot survive for much longer. Before freezing to death, she lays eggs. The eggs are not afraid of frost. When the weather turns warm next year, many baby praying mantises will emerge."

"But... But why did the wife eat the husband?"

「是公螳螂自願的，你沒看到牠都不躲嗎？」

師父說：你想想，秋天了，連蜜蜂螞蟻都要冬眠了，螳螂已經不容易找到食物，母螳螂交配之後要下蛋，好比孕婦需要進補，問題是哪兒來營養呢？為了讓下一代能夠延續，公螳螂就奉獻了自己。

"The male praying mantis was willingly eaten. Didn't you see how he did not run away?"

Master turned around to face Little Monk and said: "Think about it. It's autumn. Even the bees and ants will soon hibernate. Praying mantises cannot easily find food. The female must lay eggs after mating, and just like a pregnant woman, she needs nutrition. The problem is: where can she get nutrition? For the sake of the next generation, the male sacrificed himself.

所以世間萬物，不能只從表面看，也不能隨便論斷。千年億載、斗轉星移，能夠繁衍到今天的萬物，或是弱肉強食，或是犧牲奉獻，即使「殺」也可能隱藏了「生」的道理。

That is why for all the living beings on this earth, you cannot simply look at the surface or quickly judge them. Over hundreds of millions of years, the living beings that still live today have survived by being the strongest or by learning to sacrifice. Even in 'killing,' there are big hidden principles of 'living.' "

自損

Cutting Losses

颱颱風，禪院裡一棵大樹倒了，小沙彌驚慌地向師父報告。

「只是倒了，根還在。」師父說：「扶起來就好！」

小沙彌說：「我們扶了，樹太重，扶不動耶！」

「給它減重啊！」師父說：「把枝子鋸掉！」

「把枝子鋸掉？」小沙彌瞪大眼睛喊：「大樹已經夠可憐了！為什麼還要再傷害它？」

After a typhoon, a tree in the monastery courtyard fell. Little Monk ran to Master in a panic.

Master said: "The tree has fallen, but its roots are intact. You can set it right!"

"We've tried, but it's too heavy!" Little Monk said.

"Then saw off some branches to lighten the load!" Master said.

"Saw off some branches?" Little Monk shouted with widened eyes. "But the tree is already damaged. Why must we hurt it more?"

「倒下的樹不減重，怎麼扶？失敗的人還死要面子，怎麼東山再起？」

「把枝子先鋸掉一些，免得再被吹倒。」師父下令：「樹大招風，先自損，才能不受損。」

樹被鋸得只剩幾根大枝子，光禿禿地被扶正，怎麼看怎麼不順眼，但是才不久，禿枝上就冒出新綠，隔年居然長得跟原先一樣繁茂了。

"If a fallen tree does not cut its losses, then it cannot be set right. Similarly, if a fallen man does not set aside his ego, then he cannot make things right."

"Saw off some branches before the next typhoon," Master commanded. "Sometimes, we need to cut our losses before our losses catch up to us."

And so, the tree was set upright, with only a few branches remaining. It certainly looked odd. But before long, new leaves started to grow. A year later, the tree looked as good as the others.

走進陽光

Walk into the Sunlight

小沙彌跟師父坐車出去，天氣很不穩定。

小沙彌怨：「一下出太陽，一下陰天。」

Little Monk and Master went out in a car. The weather was quite unstable.

Little Monk complained, "It's sunny for a minute and then cloudy again!"

師父說：「不！應該說是我們一下子開進陽光裡，一下子又開出來了。太陽哪天會不出來呢？白天就算颳風下雨，它也躲在雲層後面。所以有什麼不如意，都可以看看天，告訴自己其實太陽等在那兒，就算不照過來，自己也能走進去。走進陽光裡！」

Master said: "No! We should say that we are the ones who drove into sunlight and then drove out of it. Is there ever a day when the sun does not come out? Even when there is wind and rain, the sun is hiding behind the clouds. Therefore, when things don't go your way and you feel like you're having a bad day, you can always look at the sky. Tell yourself: the sun is waiting there. Even if the sun is not shining on you, you can walk to it. Walk into the sunlight!"

放下煩惱

Put Down
the Distress

小沙彌跟師父晚上出去，山路黑，師父突然被絆了一下，向前撲倒在地上。所幸師父反應快，除了衣服沾了些塵土，沒受傷。

小沙彌把師父扶起來繼續走。

「別急！先回頭看看是什麼東西把我絆倒？」師父說。

Little Monk and Master went out at night. The mountain roads were dark. Master suddenly tripped and fell forward. Luckily, his reflexes were quick. Besides getting some dirt on his clothes, he was not hurt.

Little Monk helped Master to stand up and then continued walking.

"Don't rush! First look back and see what tripped me," Master said.

小沙彌回頭找，原來是塊大石頭。

「去你的！」小沙彌狠狠把石頭踢開。

「你把石頭踢到哪兒去了？石頭又沒錯，是我自己走路不小心，你何必生它的氣呢？」師父問：「而且你隨便踢開，會不會把別人絆倒？」

Little Monk looked behind them. It was a large rock.

"Go away!" Little Monk said, as he harshly kicked the rock away.

"To where did you kick the rock? The rock did not do anything wrong. I was the one who wasn't careful while walking. Why are you angry at the rock?" Master asked. "Besides, by kicking it away randomly, what if you cause someone else to trip?"

「我生氣！」小沙彌喊：「您怎麼不問我疼不疼呢？剛才我踢那一下，腳好疼啊！」

「你有知，它無知，你跟它生氣，能不吃虧嗎？」師父說：「你可以把石頭移開，放到它應該在的地方，譬如它是從擋土牆上掉下來的，就放回擋土牆，讓它繼續擔任擋土的工作。

"I'm angry!" Little Monk shouted. "Why don't you ask if I got hurt? My foot hurts so much from that kick!"

"You have feelings; it does not. If you get angry at it, then of course you would be at a disadvantage," Master said. "You can move the rock away and place it where it should be. For example, if it fell out of the retaining wall, then place it back in the wall, and let it continue its job of retaining soil.

如果是從山上滾下來的，就把它安置在山邊，讓它別再擋路，也別再滾動。想想！剛才你那一腳，如果把石頭踢到山下，會不會砸到人？如果把它踢到山坡上，它會不會繼續往下滾？」

「師父說那麼多，我不懂！」小沙彌嘟噥。

If it rolled down from the mountain, then place it at the side of the mountain, so that it neither blocks the road nor continues rolling. Think! If the rock fell down the mountain because of your kick, might it hit somebody? If you kicked it onto the slope, wouldn't it continue rolling?"

"Master said so much. I don't understand!" Little Monk pouted.

師父笑笑：「碰到任何煩惱，先別生氣，也別把煩惱扔給別人，你要做的是先看清楚，然後心平氣和地把煩惱拿起來，放到不再煩惱的地方。」

Master smiled. "When encountering distress, do not be quick to anger, and do not transfer your distress to other people. What you must do is to first see clearly, and then to calmly pick up the distress. Move it to a place where it will no longer be distressful."

接地氣

Down to Earth

暮冬，冰雪剛融，禪院的圍牆邊就冒出好多綠色的小葉子，過幾天，小葉子中間居然伸出花蕾，綻放了一朵朵小黃花、小紅花、小紫花。

小沙彌蹲在花圃前，很有感觸地說：「這些花好小、好漂亮！可是冬天還沒過，她們那麼嬌嫩，怎受得了呢？」

These were the last days of winter, and the land was thawing. Little green leaves had sprouted along the outer walls of the monastery. A few days later, buds appeared within the leaves, blooming into yellow, red, and purple flowers.

Little Monk crouched in front of the flowers. "The flowers look so pretty, yet so fragile! There are still some cold days ahead. How will they survive?" he asked, feeling wistful for the flowers.

師父說：「她們嬌嫩嗎？那是番紅花，別的植物連新芽都沒發出來，辛夷和櫻花也還在睡覺，這些小花卻已經探出頭了，那可不是一天兩天的工夫，表示下雪結冰的時候，她們已經在地底下一點一點往上鑽。大家還在冬眠的時候，她們已經尋求突破。」

「可不是嗎？」小沙彌喊著：「為什麼她們比大樹還厲害？」

Master said: "Do you think they are fragile? These are saffron flowers, quite different from others. While the magnolia and cherry blossoms are still asleep, these saffron flowers are awake. Under the snow and ice, they inch along day by day, so they are usually the first to break through the winter frost, before the others."

Little Monk is amazed. "Master, you don't say! These flowers are tougher than the trees? How?"

「因為她們藏在泥土深處啊！天沒暖，大地先暖。愈接地氣，愈耐寒，也愈有力量。」

"Because they stay close to the ground! The land is the first to know the changing of the seasons. The more down to earth you are, the tougher you are, and the more powerful you can be."

勝天與順天

Conquering
and Following

夜裡先是雷電交加，接著下起傾盆大雨，雨水像潑似的，禪院瞬間變成小池塘。

小沙彌急著把門關緊。

「別急著關門！先去檢查下水道，是不是被堵住了？」師父說。

小沙彌趕緊去拿傘。

The night began with thunder and lightning, then pouring rain. Water seemed to splash from the sky, and the monastery quickly turned into a small pond.

Little Monk hurriedly closed the doors shut.

"Don't rush to close the doors! First, check the drainage system. Did it get clogged?" Master said.

Little Monk hurried to get an umbrella.

「別打傘了！雨太大，打傘也沒用，還累贅。」師父說。

小沙彌衝進雨裡，一下子就回來了，邊跑邊喊：「沒堵！水不但下不去，還往外冒呢！」話沒說完，突然砰一聲，禪院的後門被撞開了，山洪像條河似的沖進來，眼看就要淹進禪房，小沙彌拿著掃把拚命往外掃，卻見師父光著膀子跑向前院，把大門打開。

"Don't use an umbrella! The rain is too heavy. An umbrella would not work but would rather burden you," Master said.

Little Monk rushed into the rain and came back quickly. He shouted while running: "It's not clogged! Water is not going down, but water is coming out!" Before he could finish speaking, suddenly with a loud boom, the monastery's back door was smashed open. Water rushed in like a river and seemed close to flooding the inner rooms. Little Monk used a broom to sweep water outward with all his might, and he saw Master running toward the front door with bare arms. Master opened the front door.

奇蹟出現了！後門進來的水，原本在院子裡愈積愈深，全由前門流了出去。

過不久，雨停了，小沙彌四處檢查，居然沒什麼損失，興奮地喊：「師父好神呦！」

It was a miracle! Water that came in through the back door was previously building up inside, but now all the water flowed out through the front door.

Soon after, the rain stopped. Little Monk checked everywhere and saw that there was not much damage. He excitedly shouted, "Master is amazing!"

「關門不管用，就把門打開。雨傘擋不住，就濯著出去。」師父笑笑：「水怎麼流進來，怎麼流出去。不能勝天，就順天！」

"If closing the door does not help, then open the door. If an umbrella cannot block the rain, then go outside without one," Master said with a smile. "Whichever way the water flows in, it will flow out the same way. When you cannot conquer fate, you can follow fate!"

黑缽的啟示

Revelation of
the Black Bowl

師父交給小沙彌一個木頭做的缽：「去！到溪邊盛一缽水回來，要滿滿一缽呦！小心走，別讓水溢出來。」

小沙彌出禪院、過田埂、下山坡，到小溪裡舀了滿滿一缽水，再往回走。

Master gave Little Monk a bowl made of wood and said, "Go! Bring back a bowl of water from the creek. Make sure it is filled to the brim! Walk carefully, and don't let the water spill."

Little Monk walked out of the monastery, across the farmland, down the hill, and to the creek. He filled the bowl with water and walked back.

邊走邊抱怨：「院子裡有方便的井水為什麼不用？非要跑那麼遠去舀溪水？」大概因為不專心，在好幾個上坡拐彎的地方，讓水溢了出去。拿給師父的時候，只剩半缽了。

隔天，師父又叫小沙彌去溪邊舀水，但是把木缽換成了瓷缽。小沙彌捧著瓷缽，到溪邊舀了滿滿一缽水，小心翼翼地走回禪房，只在爬坡時溢出一點點，得意地把接近滿缽水捧給師父。

As he walked, he silently complained: "Why couldn't I use the well that's conveniently in the monastery yard? Why did I have to come all this way to get creek water?" Perhaps because he was not paying attention, water spilled out on every uphill turn. By the time he saw Master, there was only half a bowl of water left.

The next day, Master again told Little Monk to get water from the creek, but with a porcelain bowl instead of the wooden bowl. Little Monk went to the creek and filled the porcelain bowl with water, and then he very carefully walked back, only spilling a tiny bit when climbing uphill. He proudly gave the nearly full bowl back to Master.

第三天，師父不知從哪裡掏出個黑黑髒髒的缽交給小沙彌。

「拿這個髒東西盛水？」小沙彌問。

「嫌髒，就先洗乾淨。」師父說。

小沙彌用兩根手指捏著那個髒缽，心想：「髒死了！帶臭味，還那麼重，不知以前盛什麼髒東西？師父有乾淨的缽不用，不是存心折磨我嗎？」

On the third day, Master took out a bowl that was so dirty it was black, and he gave it to Little Monk.

"We're using this dirty thing for water?" Little Monk asked.

"If you think it's too dirty, then wash it first," Master answered.

Little Monk held the dirty bowl with just two fingers and thought, "It's gross! It's smelly and heavy. Who knows what it was previously used for? Master has cleaner bowls that he's not using. Is he purposely tormenting me?"

小沙彌沒好氣地把那黑缽在溪水裡涮了涮，又用手指搓了搓，突然眼睛一亮，缽底露出一片白，不！是一片金！

小沙彌舉著缽，上氣不接下氣地跑回禪院，大喊著：「師父，這缽是金的耶！」

師父沒什麼表情，沉聲問：「水呢？」

Little Monk annoyedly rinsed the black bowl in the creek and rubbed it with his fingers. Suddenly, his eyes lit up. There was a flash of white at the bottom of the bowl. No, it was gold!

Little Monk raised up the bowl and ran back to the monastery as fast as he could. He shouted, "Master, this bowl is made of gold!"

Master was expressionless. He asked in a low voice, "Where's the water?"

小沙彌一愣：「我急著告訴您這個好消息，所以忘記舀水了！真要用金缽舀水嗎？」

Little Monk was stunned. "I was in such a hurry to tell you this good news that I forgot to scoop water! Are we really using this gold bowl to scoop water?"

「金缽舀出的水，跟木缽會有差異嗎？對你來說那是個貴重的金缽，對我來說只是個缽。無論木頭的、白瓷的、純金的，缽就是缽！」師父說：「如同我們度化人，要平等對待，不能因為世俗的尊卑貴賤而有差異。每個人都是會學習、能領悟的人，如同可以盛東西的缽，最重要的是我們要醍醐灌頂，敬謹小心地為他們注滿。」

"Is there a difference between water scooped by a gold bowl versus a wooden bowl? You seem to say that it is a valuable gold bowl, but to me, it is simply a bowl. Whether made of wood, porcelain, or pure gold, a bowl is a bowl!" said Master. "Similarly, when we enlighten people, we must treat all of them equally, with no regard for secular notions of wealth or status. Every person can learn and comprehend. The most important thing is to carefully fill each person to the brim with enlightenment, just like a bowl."

泥生蓮

Lotus in Mud

小沙彌跟師父進城，從大路進，繞小路回來。

「為什麼走小路呢？旁邊都是違建，好髒好臭。」小沙彌問。

師父沒答話，繼續走，經過一片池塘，野生的蓮花正盛開。

Little Monk and Master went into the city. They took the main road going there, but they took small side roads coming back.

"Why are we taking the side roads? There are illegal shelters here that are dirty and smelly," Little Monk asked.

Master did not answer. He continued to walk, and they passed a pond. Wild lotuses were in full bloom.

師父拍拍小沙彌：「去為師父摘一朵吧！」

小沙彌二話不說就脫掉鞋子和外褲跳進池塘，只是才走兩步就喊：「下面是稀泥耶，好黏啊！把我的腳都吸住了！」

「你要摘蓮花就別怕稀泥！一步步走穩，稀泥不會把你吃了！」

Master nudged Little Monk and said, "Pick a flower for Master!"

Little Monk did not even hesitate for a second to take off his shoes and pants to jump into the pond. But only two steps in, he hollered: "It's all slimy mud down here! So sticky! It's sucking in my feet."

"If you want to get a lotus flower, then don't be afraid of mud! Walk steadily one foot at a time. The mud won't eat you!"

小沙彌終於摘到蓮花，興奮地回到岸上遞給師父：「好香啊！好美啊！」小沙彌喊，可是跟著低頭又哇哇叫：「我腳上都是稀泥，好髒啊！」

Little Monk finally got a lotus flower, and he excitedly returned to shore to give the flower to Master. "It's fragrant! It's beautiful!" he exclaimed, but then he looked down and whined, "My feet are covered in slimy mud. So dirty!"

「洗洗就不髒了！」師父說：「不怕髒，怕你嫌髒的一顆心。我們度化人，經常是腳下踩著汙泥，手上捧著蓮花。如果你嫌髒，不願涉過泥塘，還能摘到這朵蓮花嗎？如果你嫌那些小路既髒又窄，就不進去，還能發現貧民的疾苦、幫助苦難的人們嗎？」

"Your feet will be clean again after a quick wash!" Master said. "Don't fear dirtiness. Fear your heart for its disgust toward dirtiness. When we enlighten people, we often have our feet stepping in mud and our hands holding a lotus flower. If you had felt disgusted and refused to cross the muddy pond, then could you have gotten this flower? If you feel disgusted toward narrow and dirty roads, and so you don't take them, then how can you discover the suffering of the poor and truly help the people?"

滿了嗎？

Is It Full?

小沙彌去見師父：「我已經學夠了，好像可以出師了吧！」

「什麼是夠了呢？」師父問。

「就是滿了，裝不下了。」

「那麼裝一大碗石子來吧！」

徒弟照做了。

Little Monk went to see Master and said: "I have learned enough. I think I can graduate now!"

Master asked, "What does 'enough' mean?"

"It means something is full, and you cannot put more things in."

"Then please bring over a full bowl of stones."

The apprentice did as he was told.

「滿了嗎？」師父問。

「滿了！」

師父抓來一把砂，摻入碗裡，沒有溢。

「滿了嗎？」師父又問。

「滿了！」

師父抓起一把石灰，摻入碗裡，還沒有溢。

「滿了嗎？」師父再問。

"Is it full?" Master asked.

"It's full!"

Master grabbed a handful of sand and poured it into the bowl. The bowl did not overflow.

"Is it full?" Master asked again.

"It's full!"

Master picked up a handful of garden lime and poured it into the bowl. The bowl still did not overflow.

"Is it full?" Master asked yet again.

「滿了！」

師父又倒了一盅水下去，仍然沒有溢出來。

「滿了嗎？」

「……」

"It's full!"

Master then poured a cup of water into the bowl, and still, it did not overflow.

"Is it full?"

"..."

慧根

Roots of Wisdom

過年，有信眾送來一大把晚香玉。

「拿花瓶盛水，插上，這是『歲朝清供』。」師父對小沙彌說。

過了幾天。

「給花換水了嗎？」師父問。

小沙彌搖搖頭：「要換水嗎？大殿裡的富貴竹，插兩年了，不是只要加水，不必換水嗎？」

To celebrate the New Year, a believer gave the monastery a bouquet of tuberoses.

"Fill a vase with water and put the flowers in there. These are special New Year's flowers," said Master to Little Monk.

A few days passed.

"Did you change the water in the flowers' vase?" Master asked.

Little Monk shook his head. "We have to change the water? The lucky bamboo in the hall has been there for two years. I thought we only added water and never changed water?"

「富貴竹是富貴竹，它的水不會臭。」師父說：「晚香玉是晚香玉，花雖然香，水卻會臭，不信你聞聞。」

小沙彌把瓶裡的水倒出來。「真的臭了！」小沙彌直皺眉：「為什麼它們不一樣呢？」

「因為一個能生根，一個不能生根。你看富貴竹下頭是不是長了好多根？再看看晚香玉，是不是不但沒長根，而且爛了？」

"Bamboo is bamboo. Its water will not stink," said Master. "Tuberoses are tuberoses. Although the flowers smell nice, the water eventually stinks. Take a sniff if you don't believe me."

Little Monk poured the water out of the vase. "It really does stink!" Little Monk said with a frown. "Why aren't all plants the same?"

"One can grow roots, while the other cannot. Do you see the many roots growing out from the bottom of the lucky bamboo? Now look at the tuberoses. They not only don't have roots growing out, but rather they're rotting at the bottom, right?"

師父拍拍小沙彌：「生根，是活的；不生根，是死的。」

夏天，午後總有雷雨。

禪房的一側地勢低，一下大雨就積水。

「把下面的牆板換換吧！」師父指示小沙彌：「泡太久，都朽了！」

果然靠地面的牆板，全一扯就下來了。師父抱來新的木板，兩個人一起釘上。

Master patted Little Monk and continued, "Something that takes root is alive. Something that docs not take root is dead."

That summer, there were often thunderstorms in the afternoon.

The monastery was built on a slope, and water always gathered on one side during heavy rain.

"Please change the wall panels at the bottom!" Master instructed Little Monk. "They have been soaking for too long, and they are rotting!"

Sure enough, the panels close to the ground fell off as soon as Little Monk tugged on them. Master brought over new wood panels. He and Little Monk worked on reconstructing the wall.

小沙彌一面釘一面指著旁邊的松樹問：「這是松、那也是松，這也泡水、那也泡水，為什麼松樹不爛？」

「活著不爛、死了才爛。」

秋天，禪院裡的櫻花樹突然枯了，裂開的樹皮裡爬出好多白蟻。

「怪了！春天不是還開花嗎？」小沙彌說。

As he hammered the panels, Little Monk pointed to a nearby pine tree and said, "This is pine, and that is pine too. This soaked in water, and that soaked in water too. How come the pine tree did not rot?"

"Something that is alive does not rot. It will rot only after it dies."

That autumn, the monastery's cherry blossom tree suddenly withered. Many termites crawled out of the cracked bark.

"Strange! Wasn't it just blooming this spring?" observed Little Monk.

「早上還唱歌的人，不是可能中午就死了嗎？」師父說：「死總等在那兒，就像白蟻，總等在這兒，樹爛一點，牠吃一點。你活著，牠不吃；你死了，牠就吃。死一寸、吃一寸。」

冬至，禪院裡的樹葉全掉光了，後山上也是一片寒林。傍晚，突然飄下密密的雪花。

「葉子沒了，天地就寬了。樹枝的手空了，上天就拋下白銀。」

"Someone who was singing in the morning could be dead by noon, right?" said Master. "Death is always there, just like termites. Termites are always waiting there; when the tree rots a little, they eat a little. When the tree is alive, they don't eat; when the tree dies, they eat. If one inch dies, then one inch gets eaten."

By winter solstice, the monastery's trees had lost all their leaves. The mountains' forests were also bare. That evening, dense snowflakes suddenly fell from the sky.

"When the leaves are gone, the skies are wide open. When the branches are empty-handed, the heavens toss down silver," said Master to Little Monk.

師父對小沙彌說：「看看那山上的樹，光禿禿的枝子，一個樣兒，可是裡面有多少死、多少生？多少看來死了，卻偷偷生根；多少看來活著，卻偷偷爛了。你能不警惕、不精進嗎？」

「警惕精進什麼？」小沙彌不懂。

「想想蛀蟲是不是等在旁邊！想想自己是不是正在腐爛？想想身邊的水是不是已經臭了？想想還能不能保有慧根！」

"Look at those trees on the mountain. Their bare branches all look the same, but among them, how many are dead and how many are alive? Some branches look dead, but they are secretly taking root. Some look alive, but they are secretly rotting. How can you not stay alert and constantly improve?"

"Alert about what? Improve on what?" Little Monk was confused.

"Think about whether termites are waiting nearby! Think: are you gradually rotting? Think: is your surrounding water stinking? Think about whether you can grow and preserve roots of wisdom!"

隨時、隨性、隨遇、隨緣、隨喜

Yield

三伏天，禪院中的草地枯黃了一大片。

「快撒點草種子吧！好難看哪！」小沙彌說。

「等天涼了。」師父揮揮手：「隨時！」

中秋，師父買了一包草籽，叫小沙彌去播種。

秋風起，草籽邊撒邊飄。

On the hottest day of the year, the monastery's grass was largely dry and yellow.

"Let's hurry and plant some grass seeds! This looks awful!" Little Monk said.

"Wait until the days are cooler," Master said, waving his hand. "Yield to time!"

Later in mid-autumn, Master bought a package of grass seeds and asked Little Monk to plant them.

In the autumn wind, grass seeds flew around as they were being planted.

「不好了！好多種子都被吹飛了。」小沙彌喊。

「沒關係，吹走的多半是空的，撒下去也發不了芽。」師父說：「隨性！」

撒完種子，跟著就飛來幾隻小鳥啄食。

「要命了！種子都被鳥吃了！」小沙彌急得跳腳。

"Oh no! So many seeds have been blown away!" shouted Little Monk.

"Don't worry. Most of the seeds that blew away were empty. They would not have sprouted even if they stayed on the ground," said Master. "Yield to nature!"

As soon as the seeds were all planted, a few birds flew over to eat.

"This is terrible! The birds will eat all the seeds!" Little Monk was jumping with frustration.

「沒關係！種子多，吃不完！」師父說：「隨遇！」

半夜一陣驟雨，小沙彌早晨衝進禪房：

「師父！這下真完了！好多草籽被雨沖走了！」

「沖到哪兒，就在哪兒發！」師父說：「隨緣！」

"Don't worry! There are too many seeds for the birds to eat them all," said Master. "Yield to the situation!"

There was heavy rainfall overnight. Little Monk rushed into his Master's room in the morning and shouted: "Master! It's really over now! So many seeds were washed away by the rain!"

"Wherever the seeds wash away to, they will sprout there!" said Master. "Yield to destiny!"

一個多星期過去。

原本光禿的地面，居然長出許多青翠的草苗。一些原來沒播種的角落，也泛出了綠意。

小沙彌高興得直拍手。

師父點點頭：「隨喜！」

One week passed.

Many fresh green sprouts of grass grew out of the previously bare ground. Some corners where no seeds had been planted also turned green.

Little Monk clapped with happiness.

Master nodded and said, "Yield to joy!"

點一爐好火
Light a Good Fire

不知是不是因為地球暖化，二月初，突然暖得跟春天似的，原先滿地的白雪全融化了。

「快去撿柴！」師父對小沙彌說。

「天這麼暖，還要點暖爐嗎？」小沙彌問。

「不趁天暖雪融，落在地上的枯枝露出來，難道要等再下一場雪，到雪裡挖？」

Perhaps due to global climate change, in early February, it was suddenly as warm as spring. All the snow that was covering the ground melted away.

"Hurry and go collect firewood!" Master said to Little Monk.

"It is so warm. Do we still have to light the hearth?" Little Monk asked.

"If you do not grasp the opportunity of melted snow revealing the branches on the ground, then are you going to wait until the next snowstorm and dig for branches in the snow?"

師父瞪小沙彌一眼：「天暖的時候存柴，天寒的時候燒柴；好光景存糧，壞年頭吃糧，你怎麼連這都不懂？」

果然沒過兩天，又降到冰點以下。師父帶著小沙彌，先把舊報紙揉成一團團堆在壁爐下面，放上小樹枝，再從柴房抱來大木柴，擱在頂上。

Master glared at Little Monk and said: "Store firewood when the weather is warm; burn firewood when the weather is cold. Store grain when it is a plentiful year; eat grain when it is a bad year. How do you not even know this?"

Two days later, the temperature dropped below freezing. Master taught Little Monk to first crumple up old newspapers and pile them under the fireplace, add the small branches, and then bring the big logs in from storage to place on top.

師父劃根火柴，把下面的報紙點著，延燒到小枯枝，發出啪啪的聲音，接著騰起熊熊的火焰，還不時夾著火星，像煙花盛會似的在爐子裡飛竄。

小沙彌興奮地直拍手叫好。

「叫什麼好？」師父推推小沙彌：「快把爐門關小！」

火苗一下子收斂了，小沙彌看看師父：「會熄的！」

Master lit a match and transferred thc flame to the newspaper. Then the fire reached the small branches, causing "pa pa" sounds. Next it turned into blazing flames with sparks, flying and dancing like fireworks.

Little Monk excitedly clapped his hands and cheered.

"What are you cheering for?" Master nudged Little Monk. "Hurry and close the fireplace door!"

The flames suddenly weakened. Little Monk looked at Master and said, "The fire will go out!"

「熄不了！反而會燒得更好。」

師父笑道：「火就像人間的愛情，那愛得死去活來，好像一刻也分不開的熱戀，常常來得疾也去得快。

"It won't go out! In fact, it will be an even better fire."

Master laughed and said: "Fire is just like humans' love. The kind of passionate and inseparable love that is like life and death often comes quickly but also goes away quickly.

不信你下次不關爐門，看那大火能燒多久，只怕上面的柴還沒熱，爐子已經冷卻。反不如把爐門關小，讓下面的火慢慢燒，把大塊的柴先燒透。」

果然，大木塊的邊緣漸漸冒煙、露出火苗。

「著是著了，但是火不大耶！」小沙彌說。

「不要大，要穩！夜裡夠暖就成了。」

If you don't believe me, next time don't close the fireplace door and see how long that blazing fire can last; before the logs on top even get hot, the hearth will already be cold. Instead, we are closing the fireplace door and letting the fire slowly burn from below, until the large logs are thoroughly burnt."

Sure enough, the edges of the large logs gradually emitted smoke, then sparks.

"The logs are on fire, but it's not a big fire!" said Little Monk.

"We don't want big; we want steady! It just needs to keep us warm throughout the night."

但是天沒亮，小沙彌就被凍醒。爬過去看火爐，只見幾塊黑炭，散在爐子四處。「不得了了！師父！是誰把柴動過，火都熄了。」

師父張開眼睛，看一眼：「少見多怪！那些大塊的柴，愈燒愈小，當然顯得愈來愈遠。跟人一樣，愈久愈遠，愈遠愈淡。你快用火鉗，把小炭塊攏到一起！」

However, before sunrise, Little Monk was woken up by the cold. He crawled over to the fireplace, and all he saw were a few pieces of char, scattered around the hearth. "Oh no! Master! Someone moved the wood, and now the fire is out."

Master opened his eyes and took one look. "Everything is strange to those who haven't seen much! Large logs become smaller as they burn, and therefore they seem farther and farther apart. They are just like humans who are physically apart and feel emotionally distant over time. Quickly take the fire tongs and move the small pieces of char together!"

小沙彌照辦了，看似已經熄滅的黑炭，聚成一堆，居然很快地變紅，接著竄出火苗。

「死灰復燃了！死灰復燃了！」小沙彌喊。

「胡說！死了怎麼復燃？就因為沒死，所以復燃，就因為重聚，所以重溫。快睡吧！」

Little Monk did as he was told. When the black char was gathered into a pile, the pieces quickly turned red, and then flames appeared.

"The dead ash is rekindled! The dead ash is rekindled!" Little Monk shouted.

"Nonsense! How can something that's dead be rekindled? It can only be rekindled because it never died. Reunion brings back warmth. Go to sleep!"

小沙彌醒來，天已經大亮，窗上結了一層冰，禪房裡卻挺溫暖。原來師父又添了幾塊柴，壁爐裡一片蘊藉。

「今天的火更棒了！」小沙彌說。

「今天的火不是昨天的火嗎？」師父說：「今天的火不是從昨天來的嗎？柴變了，火沒變。」

Little Monk woke up. The sky was already bright, and a layer of ice had formed on the window. But inside the room, it was warm. Apparently, Master had added more firewood, and the fireplace was full of steady heat.

"Today's fire is even better!" Little Monk said.

"Is today's fire not yesterday's fire?" said Master. "Didn't today's fire come from yesterday's fire? It is different wood, but it is the same fire."

小和尚伸個懶腰，趴著窗子往外看，接著大叫：「外面好冷啊！連小鳥都變不見了；雪好深哪！連牆都變矮了。」

師父走到窗前看了看，扶著小沙彌的肩膀：「小鳥真沒了嗎？牆真矮了嗎？這世界真變了嗎？景氣不同，世界沒變。誰不知道冬天過去就是春天？你還怕春天不來嗎？」

Little Monk stretched lazily and looked out the window. He shouted: "It's so cold outside! Even the birds have disappeared. The snow is so deep! Even the wall became shorter."

Master walked to the window, held Little Monk's shoulders and said: "Did the birds really disappear? Did the wall really become shorter? Has this world changed? The scenery is different, but it is the same world. Who doesn't know that after winter passes, spring comes? How can you fear that spring won't come?"

點一盞心燈

Light a Lamp
in the Heart

小沙彌去見師父「師父！我遁入空門已經多年，每天在這青山白雲之間，茹素禮佛、暮鼓晨鐘，經讀得愈多，心中的雜念不但不減，反而增加，怎麼辦？」

「點一盞燈，使它非但能照亮你，而且不會留下你的身影，就可以悟了！」

Little Monk went to see Master and said: "Master! I have already been in the monastery for many years. Every day, I have lived amongst the mountains and clouds, obeyed a vegetarian diet, and followed the morning clock and evening drum rituals. But no matter how much I read scripture, the chaotic thoughts in my heart are not diminishing but rather increasing. What should I do?"

"Light a lamp. Let it illuminate you, yet not make a shadow. Then you will understand!"

數十年過去⋯⋯

　　有一座禪院遠近馳名，大家都稱之為「萬燈院」，因為其中點滿了燈，成千上萬的燈，使人走入其間，彷彿步入一片燈海，燦爛輝煌。

Decades later...

There was a very famous temple, which everyone called The Temple of Ten Thousand Lamps because it was full of brightly lit lamps. When people walked in, they felt like they were entering a sea of light – brilliant and glorious.

這所萬燈院的住持，就是當年的小沙彌，雖然如今年事已高，並擁有上千的徒眾，但是他仍然不快樂，因為儘管他每做一樁功德，都點一盞燈，卻無論把燈放在腳邊、懸在頂上，乃至以一片燈海將自己團團圍住，還是總會見到自己的影子，甚至可以說：燈愈亮，影子愈顯；燈愈多，影子也愈多。

This temple's abbot was the Little Monk from years ago. Although he was now of old age and had over 1000 disciples, he was still not happy. Every time he performed an act of kindness, he lit a lamp. But regardless of whether he placed the lamp at his feet or above his head, or even when he was surrounded by a sea of lamps, he could still see his own shadow. One could say that the brighter the lamp, the clearer the shadow; the more lamps there were, the more shadows there were. He was confused, but there was no more master to ask, as his Master had passed away long ago. He himself would leave this world soon too.

他困惑了，卻已經沒有師父可以問，因為師父早已死去，自己也將不久人世。

他圓寂了，據說就在死前終於通悟。

他沒有在萬燈之間找到一生尋求的東西，卻在黑暗的禪房裡通悟：身外的成就再高，燈再亮，卻只能造成身後的影子。唯有一個方法，能使自己皎然澄澈，心無罣礙。

他點了一盞心燈！

He passed away. Supposedly right before his death, he finally understood.

He did not find what he was looking for his whole life among the ten thousand lamps, but he found it in his dark meditation room. He realized that even the greatest external accomplishments and the brightest lamps would only result in shadows. There was only one solution: purifying his soul, clearing his heart of all distractions.

He lit a lamp in his heart!

遠 足 心 靈

小沙彌
遇見
劉墉

Little Monk
Meets Yong Liu

中文·圖 —— 劉墉
英　　文 —— 劉軒、劉倚帆
編　　輯 —— 王育涵
總 編 輯 —— 李進文
執 行 長 —— 陳蕙慧

行銷總監 —— 陳雅雯
行銷企劃 —— 尹子麟、余一霞
視覺設計 —— 江孟達工作室

國家圖書館出版品預行編目 (CIP) 資料

小沙彌遇見劉墉／劉墉文.圖；劉軒,劉倚帆英譯
-- 初版 . -- 臺北市：遠足文化, 2020.05
面　；公分 . -- (心靈)
ISBN　978-986-508-062-4 (平裝)

1. 修身　　2. 通俗作品
1 9 2 . 1　　　　　　　　　　1 0 9 0 0 4 7 1 7

出 版 者 —— 遠足文化事業股份有限公司 (讀書共和國出版集團)
　　　　　　231 新北市新店區民權路 108-2 號 9 樓
　　　　　　電話 (02) 2218-1417　　傳眞 (02) 2218-0727
　　　　　　客服信箱　service@bookrep.com.tw
　　　　　　郵撥帳號　19504465
　　　　　　客服專線　0800-221-029
　　　　　　網　　址　https://www.bookrep.com.tw
　　　　　　臉書專頁　https://www.facebook.com/WalkersCulturalNo.1
　　　　　　法律顧問　華洋法律事務所　蘇文生律師
　　　　　　印　　製　呈靖彩藝有限公司

定　　價 —— 新台幣 320 元
二版一刷 —— 西元 2020 年 06 月
二版七刷 —— 西元 2023 年 12 月
Printed in Taiwan